PERSONAL IMAGES AND INSIGHTS FROM THE STARS OF FORMULA 1

VSP

Published by Vision Sports Publishing in 2014

Vision Sports Publishing Ltd
19-23 High Street
Kingston upon Thames
Surrey
KT1 1LL
www.visionsp.co.uk

ISBN: 978-1909534-19-3

Editors: Caroline Reid, Christian Sylt
Production editor: John Murray
Design: Neal Cobourne

Personality portraits and paddock photography provided by Sutton Motorsport Images
Sutton Motorsport Images is the world's largest independent motorsport picture agency. Its archive of over 4m transparencies, with a searchable on-line digital archive of over 900,000 images, spans the entire history of motorsport.
www.sutton-images.com

Printed and bound in China by Toppan Printing Co Ltd

CONTENTS

Johnny Herbert takes his photo of Damon Hill for Zoom in the paddock in Abu Dhabi (see P88).

FOREWORD

By Bernie Ecclestone

Formula 1 is the world's most watched annual sport and its drivers are known the world over. Every move they make on track is watched by millions but very few people ever get a glimpse into their lives when they aren't racing. It leaves fans guessing about questions such as what pets the drivers have, where they go on holiday and what hobbies they get up to in their free time.

This book gives a taste of what the lives of the F1 drivers and team principals are really like. Each of them has taken a photograph of anything they wanted and they are all printed on the following pages. They are views that no one else could get and they show the drivers' pets, their toys and favourite places. There are even photos taken from the podium and the drivers' parade before the race.

It has been done for a wonderful cause because the sale of this book will benefit Great Ormond Street Hospital Children's Charity and all the photos have been signed and sold at an auction in aid of it.

The F1 Group has been supporting Great Ormond Street Hospital for many years and we are proud to be able to help with the tremendous work they do. Every year the hospital treats nearly 200,000 sick children and by buying this book you are helping them keep it up. You are also getting a glimpse into a side of F1 that isn't shown on television and, as you will see, it isn't all about fast cars and champagne.

(Clockwise from top left): Kimi Räikkönen, Jacques Villeneuve, Jackie Stewart, Damon Hill and John Surtees are among the F1 world champions who signed Nikon cameras to be auctioned in aid of Great Ormond Street Hospital Children's Charity.

A MESSAGE FROM NIKON

Hidehiko Tanaka, President, Nikon UK

For any fan of Formula 1, this book is a unique opportunity to explore life behind the scenes of one of the world's most popular sports, in a series of photographs taken by some of F1's biggest names throughout the 2013 season. In fact, every single driver and team principal has contributed to this fascinating slice of F1 history.

These are shots that money can't usually buy, and every single penny they make through the sale of this book is going to the Great Ormond Street Hospital Children's Charity. The hospital, a world leader in treating sick children, needs to raise £50 million a year in order to build state-of-the-art facilities, develop new treatments and save more children's lives, and charity projects like this are vital to its continued success.

I am delighted that Nikon UK has been able to play a part in this very worthwhile project by supplying the cameras used to capture some of these remarkable images of day-to-day life on the F1 tour circuit. As a fan of Formula 1 myself, and a passionate photographer, I'm honoured to have one of my own shots included in the book, too, taken at the British Grand Prix at Silverstone (see P104).

In a charity first, we've also had seven Nikon COOLPIX S9500 cameras signed by seven world champions – Sebastian Vettel, Kimi Räikkönen, Damon Hill, Jacques Villeneuve, John Surtees, Alain Prost and Sir Jackie Stewart – to be auctioned alongside many of the photographs.

At Nikon we're not only passionate about imaging and enabling people to capture amazing moments and memories, like those in this book, but we firmly believe in the importance of contributing to the communities we're based in, and there could be no better cause for any of us to support than Great Ormond Street Hospital Children's Charity.

So a heartfelt thank you for buying your copy and playing your own valuable part in helping Great Ormond Street continue to care for over 200,000 sick children every year – and I hope you enjoy the photographs as much as I have and as much as the F1 drivers and team principals did taking them.

At the heart of the image **Nikon**

INTRODUCTION

Zoom started with a very simple idea. Christian Sylt and Caroline Reid, authors of Formula 1's industry monitor *Formula Money*, realised that although there are many charity auctions in sport they all tend to follow a similar pattern. The items on offer are usually signed photos of the athletes or signed kit that they use. They often raise a great deal of money but, despite carrying an autograph, the items tell the buyer little new about the sports star who signed them. *Zoom* was put in motion to rectify that by turning the tables and asking all the drivers and team principals in F1 to take photographs which would then be signed and put up for auction.

There had never before been an auction of signed photos taken by the stars of any sport and several things were crucial to making it happen. The first was gaining support from the world-renowned Great Ormond Street Hospital which has had a long association with F1. It was chosen to receive the proceeds from the auction and it loved the unique concept behind *Zoom*. Next Coys, the top motoring auction house, agreed to handle the sale.

PG BRUNELLI

One of the most important steps in establishing *Zoom* was the final one and this was getting the support of F1's chief executive, Bernie Ecclestone, who Christian has known for a decade. Bernie's support has been invaluable and the participation of all the drivers and team principals soon followed. Such has been the level of interest in *Zoom* that former F1 drivers and champions, as well as commentators and designers, have all participated.

The first auction took place in London in September 2012 and was a resounding success. The star-studded event was attended by celebrities, VIPs and the stars of F1 and was so popular that a second edition of *Zoom* was launched, showcasing the photographic talents of the 2013 grid.

All the photographers took to the challenge with gusto, resulting in a diverse group of photos which shows both insider views from the track and personal pictures which have nothing to do with racing. This collection of photos doesn't just give a glimpse into the lives of F1's superstars, it reveals what drives them.

There is a truly international aspect to the photographs, with images taken in locations ranging from the tops of mountains to the shores of the sea, from the foot of the statue of Christ the Redeemer in Rio to a Rolling Stones concert in Montreal, from Michael Schumacher's peaceful train ride through Switzerland to Fernando Alonso's shot of the frenzied Monza crowd taken from the podium itself.

In an added twist from the previous event, some of the sport's greatest drivers have also signed a set of COOLPIX S9500 cameras kindly provided for *Zoom* by Nikon. It is the first time that cameras signed by F1 world champions have been auctioned and the signatories cover six decades of F1 history: Sebastian Vettel, Kimi Räikkönen, Damon Hill, Jacques Villeneuve, John Surtees, Alain Prost and Sir Jackie Stewart.

All the F1 teams, team bosses and drivers have played a key part in making this happen and we sincerely thank them along with everyone else who has donated a photo. We would also like to thank *Zoom*'s partners: Nikon, Bahrain International Circuit, Coys, the InterContinental London Park Lane, Kingfisher Beer, Vision Sports Publishing, Arena Imaging and Sutton Motorsport Images, as well as Outside Organisation, Christine Gorham and Inga Stracke who helped make this event possible.

Special thanks need to go to Bernie and Great Ormond Street Hospital. We are proud to be a part of helping them continue with the tremendous work they do.

Caroline Reid and Christian Sylt, December 2013

Sebastian Vettel only turned 26 in 2013 but is already one of the most decorated drivers in the history of the sport. He became the youngest ever driver to score a point on his debut with BMW in 2007 at age 19, and by 21 he was the youngest ever driver to win a race with victory at the 2008 Italian Grand Prix for Toro Rosso. He switched to Red Bull Racing for 2009 when he finished second in the championship and followed it up with four consecutive world titles between 2010 and 2013 – putting him joint third in the list of F1 greats at the tender age of 26.

2013 TEAM: Red Bull Racing
NATIONALITY: German

SEBASTIAN VETTEL

Freedom

"I enjoy the mountains very much, they give me a lot of freedom and many possibilities for sports activities. It's especially great in winter time when I can go skiing. The Red Wall in Austria's Vorarlberg is awesome. I went there with my family for my first ever skiing trip and just love to come back there. I feel at home and can relax and enjoy!"

Mark Webber showed his star potential right from the start of his F1 career, scoring a miraculous fifth place on his debut at the 2002 Australian Grand Prix, racing a Minardi car in which it was often an achievement just to qualify. After a few years in cars that didn't match his talent, the Australian joined Red Bull Racing in 2007, but was initially hit by more disappointment and reliability woes. Finally, after 130 races he scored his first victory at the 2009 German Grand Prix and didn't stop there. He retired from F1 at the end of 2013 with an enviable CV.

2013 TEAM: Red Bull Racing
NATIONALITY: Australian

MARK WEBBER

A Mountain View

"This is a shot I took while cycling in the French Alps during the F1 break."

PIRELLI

Fernando Alonso is now known as one of the most successful drivers in F1, but it wasn't always an easy ride. He started his F1 career in 2001 driving for Minardi, a team that was synonymous with failure, but still managed to impress the sport's power brokers. By 2003 he was behind the wheel of a Renault and took his first victory at the Hungarian Grand Prix. World championships followed in 2005, then again in 2006, making him one of a rare elite to win back-to-back titles. Alonso made the switch to Ferrari in 2010, bringing together two of the biggest names in the sport.

2013 TEAM: Ferrari
NATIONALITY: Spanish

FERNANDO ALONSO

A Special Feeling

"I took this photo on the podium at the 2013 Italian Grand Prix. Stepping onto the Monza podium is always a special feeling, as it's the only one where you can feel all the love that the fans have for the team and it's the best prize at the end of the weekend."

Shell LEGO Challenge
#shellLEGOchallenge
Santander
KASPERSKY

Felipe Massa's F1 career has been dominated by two unlucky incidents. The first came in the final round of the 2008 championship at his home Brazilian Grand Prix. Massa took the chequered flag for victory and it seemed to everyone that he had also won the championship. However, Timo Glock ran wide on the last corner, allowing title rival Lewis Hamilton to gain one place and take the championship by a single point. Then, just months later, Massa was seriously injured when a stray suspension spring from another car burst through his visor. He returned to F1 the next year.

2013 TEAM: Ferrari
NATIONALITY: Brazilian

FELIPE MASSA

Memories to Treasure

"My team-mates – a great memory from my time at Ferrari. I've had some great times, some difficult times as well. You would always prefer great results, great things rather than difficult things, but I've learned a lot from everything I've done at Ferrari."

vodafone
MERCEDES

Jenson Button's F1 career has been a rollercoaster ride. Hailed as a great talent on his debut for Williams in 2000, he spent several years in the wilderness when he constantly seemed to be driving for the wrong team at the wrong time. Despite his talent, he had to wait until his 113th race before his first win, for Honda at the chaotic 2006 Hungarian Grand Prix. Honda exited its backing for 2009, but against all odds Button's patience paid off and he was finally rewarded with an unexpected world championship. Button has since switched to McLaren where he has continued his race-winning form.

2013 TEAM: McLaren
NATIONALITY: British

JENSON BUTTON

My Team

"Thanks for your hard work, guys!"

Sergio Pérez was hailed as a star of the future when he moved into F1 in 2011. The talented Mexican took multiple points finishes in his first season in F1 for Sauber, but his second turned out even better. At the second race of the season, the Malaysian Grand Prix, he finished second and for a time it looked like he might even overtake Fernando Alonso's Ferrari for victory. Another podium followed at the Canadian Grand Prix, despite Pérez starting only in 15th, which was enough to net him a coveted seat with McLaren for 2013.

2013 TEAM: McLaren
NATIONALITY: Mexican

SERGIO PÉREZ

A Dog's Life

"My dog, Canelo, enjoying a float in the pool."

'Iceman' Kimi Räikkönen stunned the motorsport world when he was given his debut F1 drive for Sauber in 2001. The Finn had previously competed in just 23 races but took sixth place in his first race and by 2003 had claimed his first win for McLaren, finishing the championship in second place. He switched to Ferrari for 2007, winning the championship at the final race, but when the results dried up he sensationally quit F1 at the end of 2009 for the World Rally Championship. By 2012 he was back in F1 at the wheel of a Lotus. He returned to Ferrari in 2014.

2013 TEAM: Lotus
NATIONALITY: Finnish

KIMI RÄIKKÖNEN

Back to Nature

“After a busy F1 weekend, I like to relax away from everything. The natural world is very peaceful to me.”

Romain Grosjean got his first taste of F1 in 2009, when he was drafted into Renault for seven races. The best he managed was a 13th place and he wasn't retained for 2010. He turned to junior series GP2, taking the championship in 2010, and was back as an F1 test driver with his old team in 2011. Few people seriously expected he would get another shot at F1 proper and there was widespread surprise when he was signed as a race driver for Renault, now renamed Lotus, in 2012. The surprise grew when Grosjean delivered one stunning performance after another, making him a firm fan favourite.

2013 TEAM: Lotus
NATIONALITY: French

ROMAIN GROSJEAN

A Different Side of Tokyo

"Tokyo can be a very busy, active city and I normally prefer peaceful places, but visiting it for the first time in 2012 I fell in love with the city. It's beautiful to walk through the different places and discover so much culture. On the other side, Tokyo Bay looks very quiet from the bridge and that's the contrast I like about the city. I'm looking forward to going back there one day – why not with my little man Sacha?"

Nico Rosberg's father Keke was F1 world champion in 1982 and the junior Rosberg made his own debut in 2006 driving for his dad's old team, Williams. From the start he showed he had inherited some of his father's skill and at his first race he became the youngest ever driver to set a fastest lap. He scored his first podium at the 2008 Australian Grand Prix. For 2010 he moved to the revived works Mercedes team which brought him regular podium places and in 2012 he finally took his first victory. More wins followed in 2013, establishing him as one of the men to beat.

2013 TEAM: Mercedes
NATIONALITY: German

NICO ROSBERG

Special Vintage "At the wheel of the 1938 W 154 at Stuttgart. Self portrait."

Lewis Hamilton began his F1 career at an early age. At just 13, his performances in karts drew the attention of McLaren founder Ron Dennis, who was so impressed he signed the youngster up to McLaren's junior driver programme and included an option that if Hamilton ever made it to F1, McLaren would get first refusal on his services. Nine years later he became an F1 driver at McLaren and in 2008 he took the world title in a thrilling last-lap conclusion to the championship. It made him at that time the youngest ever world champion at the age of just 23. He switched to Mercedes for 2013.

2013 TEAM: Mercedes
NATIONALITY: British

LEWIS HAMILTON

Christ the Redeemer

"Brazil is the last race in the calendar each year. It's also the home of my idol, Ayrton Senna, so coming back here every November is really special and makes me realise how privileged I am and how much I have to be grateful for. This year I stopped off in Rio before going to the track and visited the Christ the Redeemer statue. It's amazing how this statue looks over, and after, the whole city and the view is incredible. These moments remind me how blessed I am to have the best job in the world. God is the greatest."

MARINA BAY
100
F

Nico Hülkenberg made his Formula 1 debut for Williams in 2010 and gained several points finishes and a stunning pole position in a car that was far from the class of the field. However, the team needed drivers that could bring in sponsorship as well as points and Hülkenberg was dropped for 2011. He moved to Force India as their test driver and was rewarded with a race seat for 2012. At the wheel of the Force India he regularly featured in the top 10 and scored a career-best finish of fourth place at the Belgian Grand Prix, earning himself a place at Sauber for 2013.

2013 TEAM: Sauber
NATIONALITY: German

NICO HÜLKENBERG

A Night-time Stroll

"I took this picture during my track walk in Singapore. It shows the Anderson Bridge after which you go into a very tight hairpin. You can see how bright the circuit is lit for the night race. It is the only night race of the year and in addition it is on a street circuit right in the heart of Singapore. The track is very thrilling to drive, especially in qualifying when you get closer and closer to the walls."

Mexico's Esteban Gutiérrez came to F1 as a rookie in 2013, with an impressive record in junior formulae. After rising through the young driver talent programme of local telecoms giant, Telmex, he headed off to race in Europe, competing in Formula BMW and Formula Three before becoming the inaugural champion of the new GP3 series in 2010, winning 10 races out of 16. He made the step up to GP2 for 2011, where he won four races before getting a drive with Sauber for 2013. He scored his first points at the Japanese Grand Prix with an impressive drive to seventh place.

2013 TEAM: Sauber
NATIONALITY: Mexican

ESTEBAN GUTIÉRREZ

A Perfect Sunset

"To watch the sunset is one of my favorite activities during my free time, because it relaxes me and brings me peace."

100

Paul di Resta comes from a racing family. His cousin is three-times Indianapolis 500 winner Dario Franchitti and there are also other racers in the family, although Di Resta is the first to make it into Formula 1. He had a successful pre-F1 career, winning the Formula Three Euroseries and DTM titles, before earning a drive for Force India in 2011. Since then he has secured a string of good points finishes and has been tipped as a future race winner.

2013 TEAM: Force India
NATIONALITY: British

PAUL DI RESTA

On Parade in Singapore

"I took this photo during the drivers' parade in Singapore. It's a rare moment before the race when you really get to soak up the atmosphere and feel the buzz from the fans. It's one of the best events of the year and this photo helps sum up the spectacular nature and challenge of the track."

Adrian Sutil made his Formula 1 debut in 2007 for the Spyker team and scored the only point of the team's brief F1 career at the Japanese Grand Prix. By the end of the year it had been bought out by Indian billionaire Vijay Mallya and renamed Force India but Sutil stayed on. At first points were hard to come by, but at the 2009 Italian Grand Prix Sutil scored a stunning fourth place, taking the fastest lap in the process. More strong points finishes followed in 2010 and 2011 and, on his return to the team in 2013, he scored an impressive fifth place in the Monaco Grand Prix.

2013 TEAM: Force India
NATIONALITY: German

ADRIAN SUTIL

Alpine Retreat

"I took this picture during a tour through the Swiss Alps. It combines all of my passions: nature, cars, driving, the Alps, Switzerland and home. It's here that I come to restore my energy levels after a busy weekend of Formula 1."

When Pastor Maldonado first entered F1 in 2011 with Williams there were many observers who doubted he was the right driver for the job. He brought with him a substantial sponsorship package from Venezuelan oil company PDVSA and this was believed to be instrumental in the decision to sign him rather than keep the existing driver line-up. However, all that was put behind him when he surged to victory in the 2012 Spanish Grand Prix, the first Venezuelan to win a race in F1 and the first win for Williams in almost eight years.

2013 TEAM: Williams
NATIONALITY: Venezuelan

PASTOR MALDONADO

Venezuelan Paradise

"I took this photo in Los Roques in Venezuela. It is a collection of islands on the Caribbean coast with the most beautiful beaches. I always go there to relax and have been visiting for many years with my family. It's one of my favourite places to go in the world."

What makes Finns such good racing drivers? Valtteri Bottas is the latest in a long line of talent from the Scandinavian country and is looking to follow in the footsteps of famous predecessors such as Keke Rosberg, Mika Häkkinen and Kimi Räikkönen. He came to F1 with an impressive junior series record, winning GP3 in 2011 and twice taking the prestigious Formula Three Masters title at Zandvoort. Williams snapped him up as their test driver in 2012, before promoting him to a race seat in 2013.

2013 TEAM: Williams
NATIONALITY: Finnish

VALTTERI BOTTAS

The Perfect Place to Relax

"I took this picture in the August break when I went back to Finland. This is near my hometown of Nastola, and it shows the calm and quiet Finnish lakeside well – the perfect place to relax."

Red Bull
NOVA
Chemicals
CEPSA
RADIO
PIT
LIM
DRS
FAIL
x1
PC
BPF
BBAL
N
R

Jean-Eric Vergne established his reputation in British Formula Three, winning the 2010 championship with 13 race victories. It drew the attention of Formula 1 teams and in 2011 he was appointed as a test driver for Toro Rosso. This changed into a race drive for 2012 and he made his debut at the season opener, the Australian Grand Prix. He just missed out on a points finish, but managed to score at the following race in Malaysia and followed this up with more points in Belgium later in the season. He achieved a career-best sixth place at the 2013 Canadian Grand Prix.

2013 TEAM: Toro Rosso
NATIONALITY: French

JEAN-ERIC VERGNE

Lucky Mascot

“Here's my lion friend who spends every session watching me from the back of the garage. I brought him along to scare off the black cat that has brought me too much bad luck this year. He's the right animal for the job, as my engineers call me Simba, because they say I have the driving style of a lion.”

Daniel Ricciardo made his mark pre-F1 by following in the footsteps of many of the greats by winning the prestigious British Formula Three championship. It caught the eye of Formula 1 bosses and for 2010 he was appointed as a test driver at Toro Rosso. The team saw him as a future race driver and helped steer him into an HRT drive for the second half of 2011, where he impressed with some solid drives. Toro Rosso signed him for a race drive in 2012 and he scored points on his first outing at his home race, the Australian Grand Prix.

2013 TEAM: Toro Rosso
NATIONALITY: Australian

DANIEL RICCIARDO

Musical Memories

“This was at Download Festival in 2013. I got to see one of my favourite bands, The Gaslight Anthem, perform backstage. Such a good day with great memories. Music is a big part of my life.”

sparco
intel
CATERHAM
ENG 0 STOP
BO
REV
PIT
TORQUE
OFF
KERS
WING
ACK
TALK
MIX
CATERHAM
DRINK
SC
MID
CLUTCH
ENTRY
N
LAUNCH
OIL
RAIN

Charles Pic was exposed to motor racing from an early age as his godfather is former F1 driver Eric Bernard. After a spell in junior series in France he moved into GP2 for 2010 and 2011, winning three races in the championship plus another in its GP2 Asia spin-off series. The performance impressed Marussia, who signed him to race in F1 in 2012, and he showed his potential at the Belgian Grand Prix when he finished top in a free practice session, a rare feat for one of the smaller teams. He switched to Caterham for 2013.

2013 TEAM: Caterham
NATIONALITY: French

CHARLES PIC

On the Grid at Monza

“This is the view from my cockpit on the grid in Monza.”

EADS
EADS
RENAULT
CATERHAM
CATERHAM
McGREGOR
imagination at work
AIRBUS
PIRELLI
Air Asia
EQ8
Regus
DELL

At 28 years old when the 2013 season began, Giedo van der Garde was old for an F1 rookie, already two years older than the age at which Sebastian Vettel has won four world titles. For a long time it had looked like he would never get his chance as test drives for Spyker and Force India in 2007 and 2008 had both come to nothing, leaving him to spend four seasons in GP2. However, when he took a race victory in the series for the first time in 2012, Caterham gave him the chance to step up to an F1 race drive for 2013.

2013 TEAM: Caterham
NATIONALITY: Dutch

GIEDO VAN DER GARDE

Behind the Scenes

"My race team crew, Japan 2013. From left to right: Juan Ramirez, Damian Le Breuilly, Mike Horn, Chris Bethell, Jim Duffy, Alan Lear (eyes shut!), Brian Brown, Dennis Fortune and George Lancaster."

Bifold

Widely touted as a star of the future, Jules Bianchi has racing in his blood. His grandfather Mauro was a world champion sportscar racer and his great-uncle Lucien was a Le Mans winner who scored a podium at the 1968 Monaco Grand Prix for Cooper. Bianchi Junior has already impressed the powers that be in the sport and, despite being in a car that isn't the fastest on the grid, has shown real promise in 2013, his debut year in F1.

2013 TEAM: Marussia
NATIONALITY: French

JULES BIANCHI

My Crew at Work

"My car crew. A great bunch of guys who are rarely in the limelight, but deserve it more than anyone for all their hard work behind the scenes."

PAN PACIFIC

Max Chilton is the latest in a long line of British racing drivers to make it to the wheel of an F1 car. Chilton built up a competitive junior series record with wins in British Formula Three and GP2 Series and got his first taste of F1 as Marussia's test driver in 2012. The team decided to promote him to a race drive in 2013 and although he didn't have a chance to fight the big names he impressed in other ways, becoming the first driver in history to make it to the finish line in his first 17 races.

2013 TEAM: Marussia
NATIONALITY: British

MAX CHILTON

Singapore at Night

"Singapore. Wow, what a Grand Prix circuit! The only way to view it – at night! I won there in GP2 in 2012 so returning for my F1 debut this year was really special."

Christian Horner started out in motorsport as a driver, but soon realised that he didn't have the speed necessary to make it to the top. He decided to continue with Arden, the team he had set up to further his own career in Formula 3000. In 2003 and 2004 Arden took the F3000 championship and Horner's management skills caught the eye of Red Bull boss, Dietrich Mateschitz. He installed Horner as team principal of the new Red Bull Racing. Horner has led Red Bull to both drivers' and constructors' world championships for four years in a row from 2010 to 2013.

Red Bull team principal
NATIONALITY: British

CHRISTIAN HORNER

Bobby and Betsy

"This is a photo of my two miniature donkeys. Bobby is on the left and it's Betsy close up!"

PUMA
FERNANDO ALONSO
Santander
SCUDERIA FERRARI
PUMA
Santander
SCUDERIA FERRARI
Santander

Stefano Domenicali joined Ferrari straight from university, working in the car company's accounts department. Within a year he had the chance to follow his love of motor racing when he became race director at Ferrari's Mugello circuit where he organised events for series such as MotoGP and DTM. He fulfilled his dream when he moved to the Ferrari F1 team in 1995 and a year later became team manager. He rose steadily through the ranks until he was appointed as team principal in 2008. Under his leadership, Ferrari won the 2008 constructors' championship and has consistently finished on the podium since then.

Ferrari team principal
NATIONALITY: Italian

STEFANO DOMENICALI

Great People, Great Team

"Our drivers, together. In this sport teamwork is the most important thing and in Ferrari, we have a great team, made up of people who are progressing together and who can now show what they are capable of."

14
vodafone
VODAFONE

Unlike most of his contemporaries, Martin Whitmarsh worked outside motorsport for several years before coming into F1. He was manufacturing director at British Aerospace, in charge of Hawk and Harrier airframe production, before he moved to McLaren as head of operations in 1989. In 1997 he was promoted to managing director at the team and held several senior positions before he became team principal in 2009 following the retirement of Ron Dennis. Under Whitmarsh's leadership the team has frequently been on winning form.

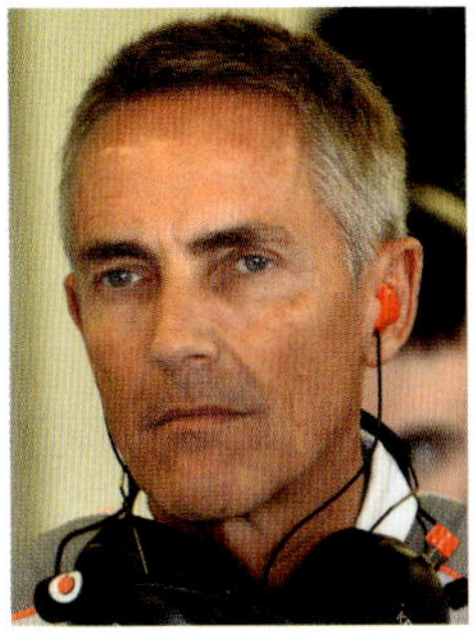

McLaren team principal

NATIONALITY: British

MARTIN WHITMARSH

Data Analysis "Our engineers going through the data post session."

Eric Boullier moved into motorsport as chief engineer at the Spanish junior series competitor, Racing Engineering. Before long he had been snapped up by French rival DAMS as its managing and technical director. Boullier was also chief executive of young driver promoter, Gravity Sport Management. When Gravity bought a stake in the Renault F1 team in 2009, he was installed as team principal. The team has since changed its name to Lotus and with Boullier at the helm has impressed many, with several race victories in 2012 and 2013.

Lotus team principal
NATIONALITY: French

ERIC BOULLIER

Paradise Beach “Relaxing away from the track – a paradise by the sea.”

Toto Wolff started out in motorsport as a driver, racing in Formula Ford and sports cars in the 1990s and early 2000s. Alongside his motorsport interests he set up an investment company, Marchfifteen, initially focusing on technology companies. It was a great success and allowed him to fuel his motorsport ambitions, investing in German racing team HWA in 2006 and then the Williams F1 team in 2009. In 2013, he became executive director at the Mercedes team, acquiring a 30 per cent stake. He is married to Williams test driver Susie Wolff.

Mercedes executive director
NATIONALITY: Austrian

TOTO WOLFF

Iconic Design

“Taken earlier this year in Affalterbach, home of AMG. This symbolizes not just the power of the Mercedes brand, combining design and performance, but also (via the iconic Gullwing design) the history I have taken on in leading Mercedes-Benz motorsport activities.”

As F1's first female team principal, Monisha Kaltenborn occupies a special place in the sport's history. She worked for various legal firms before becoming the in-house lawyer at the Fritz Kaiser Group (FKG) in 1998. FKG had just become a part-owner of Sauber and Kaltenborn got her first taste of F1 when she was put in place to oversee its legal affairs. When FKG sold its shares in 2000 she stayed on and was appointed to the board the next year. Following team founder Peter Sauber's retirement in 2012 she became team principal and 33 per cent owner of the Swiss outfit.

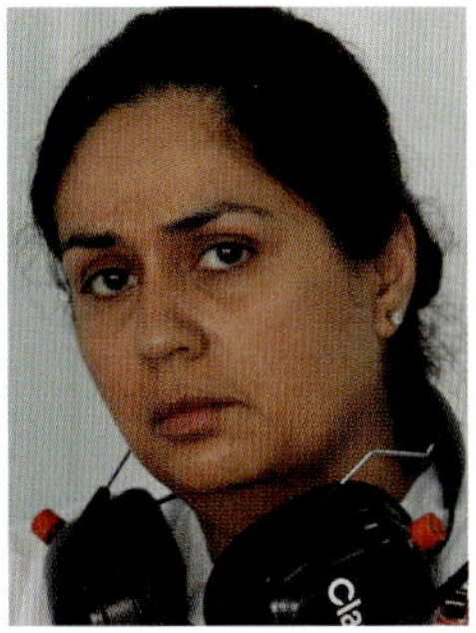

Sauber team principal
NATIONALITY: Indian/Austrian

MONISHA KALTENBORN

Sailing on Lake Zürich

“This is the view you get when crossing Lake Zürich from Küsnacht to Thalwil. On a beautiful day like this you can see the Alps in the back and enjoy the afternoon with family and friends.”

mobile
KINGFISHER
SAHARA Force India
TW STEEL
saharaforceindia.com

Flamboyant Indian billionaire Vijay Mallya has been a fan of motorsport since his childhood and became a Formula 1 team owner in 2007 when he bought the Spyker team, renaming it Force India. The team had hit on hard times and scored no points in 2008. Under Mallya's leadership Force India slowly turned its fortunes around and in 2011 finished the championship in sixth place, by far the best performance of the smaller teams. Away from the track, Mallya collects artefacts associated with Indian history, including a Rolls-Royce garbage truck that once belonged to a maharajah.

Force India team principal
NATIONALITY: Indian

VIJAY MALLYA

Ready to Race

"The formation of the grid is one of the most special and intense moments of a race weekend. It's a busy place full of anticipation and expectation. In Monza this year I took the opportunity to take a photo of Paul as he prepares for the start of the race."

PLEASE
KEEP OFF THE
GRAVEL

As the daughter of Williams founder Sir Frank Williams, Claire Williams has racing in her blood. She followed in the family footsteps after leaving university when her first job was as a press officer at Silverstone. She then joined the family business the following year. After working her way up through the marketing and communications department Williams was appointed deputy team principal in 2013, taking a more pivotal role in its day-to-day operations. She is determined to help guide Williams to the top of F1 again.

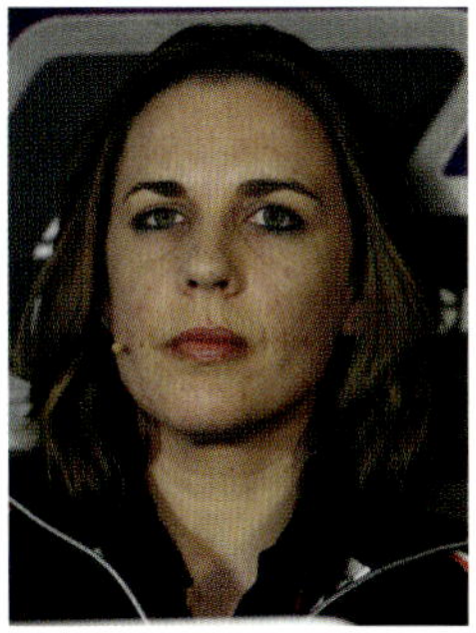

Williams deputy team principal
NATIONALITY: British

CLAIRE WILLIAMS

Green Machine

"I photographed our latest topiary in the grounds at the Williams factory in Grove. When King & Co. approached us to create something for the Chelsea Flower Show in 2012, they took inspiration from our original topiary but created and grew their own. We worked with them for about a year before we took it to Chelsea, and it was incredibly well received and successful, winning a gold medal. Frank loves England and loves landscaping and gardens – it's a passion he and Mum shared. We are proud to have our topiary cars here, and they are in honour of Ginny which makes them even more important to us now."

SCUDERIA TORO ROSSO
33
PIRELLI

Franz Tost's first foray into motorsport was as a driver, but although he won the 1983 Austrian FF Championship, he felt he would never reach the top and instead took a sports management degree. He worked for Ralf Schumacher's management team, looking after the driver's interests at Jordan and Williams before becoming the operations manager of BMW's F1 programme. When Toro Rosso was launched in 2006 he was appointed team principal and has managed the team since then, inspiring it to a first victory at the 2008 Italian Grand Prix.

Toro Rosso team principal
NATIONALITY: Austrian

FRANZ TOST

Practice Makes Perfect

"I took this photo in Singapore this year. As the only night race on the calendar it represents the sport's ability to think of new ways to make the overall show more interesting. The guys here are carrying out one of the thousands of practice pit stops they do during the course of a season and it highlights key elements of the sport, namely speed, precision and teamwork."

As F1's newest team principal in 2013, Cyril Abiteboul has a tough job. The Frenchman started work for Renault back in 2001 before becoming business development manager at their F1 team in 2007. He was subsequently appointed executive director of Renault Sport F1, where he came into contact with Caterham as an engine supplier in 2011. Abiteboul joined the team in 2012 and, when founder Tony Fernandes handed over the wheel at the end of the year, he became part of an elite group of people who have led an F1 team.

Caterham team principal
NATIONALITY: French

CYRIL ABITEBOUL

Positive Forecast "When I look up and see clouds I think this may be our day…"

After a brief career racing junior single seaters, which included a victory in Formula Ford, in 1990 John Booth set up Manor Motorsport initially to compete in Formula Renault. By 1999, the successful outfit had graduated to the British Formula Three championship, where it won the title at its first attempt. Manor launched the careers of a host of F1 stars, including Lewis Hamilton, Kimi Räikkönen and Paul di Resta, and won its own entry into F1 in 2010, competing first under Virgin branding, then as Marussia.

Marussia team principal
NATIONALITY: British

JOHN BOOTH

F1's Biggest Wheel "An iconic symbol of the best race circuit in the world – Suzuka!"

Unlike most top team bosses, Flavio Briatore did not have a background in motorsport or engineering when he came to F1. He had been working for Benetton in America when Luciano Benetton moved him into the unfamiliar world of F1. He built up a super-team for Benetton in the mid-1990s. Michael Schumacher won the drivers' title in 1994 and 1995 with Benetton also taking the constructors' title in the latter year. Briatore led the team, rebadged as Renault, to further success with Fernando Alonso's world titles in 2005 and 2006.

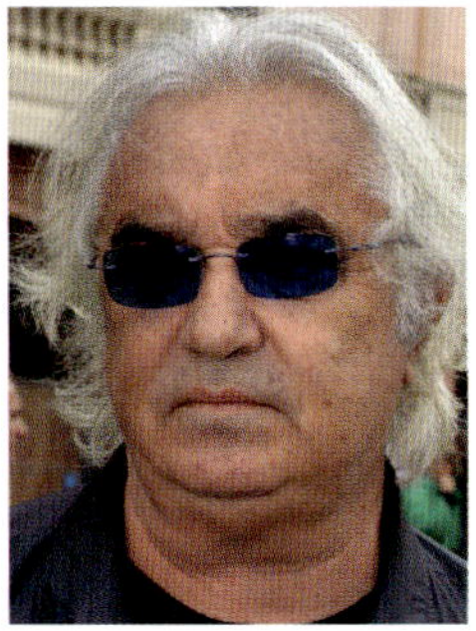

Former F1 championship-winning team principal
NATIONALITY: Italian

FLAVIO BRIATORE

Bird's-eye View “We have a visitor this morning on the balcony. Monte Carlo, October 2013.”

Although most recognised nowadays as a well-respected TV commentator, Martin Brundle is arguably one of the best F1 drivers never to have won a race. During an F1 career that spanned from 1984 to 1996 he raced for teams including McLaren, Williams, Benetton, Brabham and Jordan, finishing on the podium nine times, including second places at the 1992 Italian and 1994 Monaco Grands Prix. However, his racing highlight came outside F1 when he led Jaguar to victory in the 1990 24 Hours of Le Mans.

Former F1 driver and Sky F1 commentator
NATIONALITY: British

MARTIN BRUNDLE

Wear and Tear “Kimi's front Pirelli after he spun off in Suzuka.”

James Calado is considered by many to be the next big British star in F1 and his career has been backed by the young driver programme, the Racing Steps Foundation. After a successful career in karting, he impressed first in Formula Renault and then in Formula Three and GP3 before he made the switch to F1's immediate feeder series GP2, winning his first event in Abu Dhabi in 2011. He won twice the following year and on another couple of occasions in 2013. Force India was clearly impressed and snapped him up as a test driver from the 2013 Italian Grand Prix onwards.

Force India test driver
NATIONALITY: British

JAMES CALADO

A Very Special Track

"I took this photo at Suzuka, standing on the main straight looking towards turn one. It's a very special track with incredible corners and is also the scene of some of the most memorable moments in Formula 1 history."

Popular driver Karun Chandhok had a successful career in junior series, including GP2 and A1 Grand Prix, before making the break into F1 with HRT in 2010. He was reserve driver for Team Lotus in 2011, but particularly among British fans is probably most fondly recognised for his extremely knowledgeable and witty commentary for BBC Radio 5 Live. In 2012 he turned to sports cars when he entered the inaugural FIA World Endurance Championship and racked up an impressive sixth place at the Le Mans 24 Hour race on his first attempt.

Former driver
NATIONALITY: Indian

KARUN CHANDHOK

On the Border

“I went to the ‘Wagah border’, which is the official border between India and Pakistan, this year for the first time. The gates between the two countries open only for a few minutes every day and there’s a big ceremony at 4:30pm every evening when they take down the flags for the night. A very special place!”

Award-winning actor Liam Cunningham is a familiar face in the Formula 1 paddock and manages to fit in several races a year around his busy filming schedule. He is best known for his roles as reformed smuggler Davos Seaworth in TV series *Game of Thrones* and pilot Mad Dog Maguire in *The Mummy: Tomb of the Dragon Emperor*. He has also acted in films including *Clash of the Titans, The Wind That Shakes the Barley* and *A Little Princess* and won a BAFTA for his role in crime short, *Pitch Black Heist*.

Actor and F1 fan
NATIONALITY: Irish

LIAM CUNNINGHAM

The Trophy “Nico Rosberg's winning trophy at the 2013 British Grand Prix.”

Bernie Ecclestone was involved in F1 long before its current drivers were born. After failing to qualify for the 1958 Monaco and British Grands Prix he switched to driver management where he found the perfect outlet for his business skills. In 1972 he became owner of the Brabham team and got involved in the political and financial negotiations that dogged the sport. This culminated in 1981 with the signing of the first Concorde Agreement, which contracted the teams to race and set out the division of revenues. This enabled Ecclestone to transform F1 into a world-class television spectacle.

Formula 1 Group chief executive
NATIONALITY: British

BERNIE ECCLESTONE

Room With a View

“This is the view from my house in Gstaad in summer. I have had the house for 25 years. I like looking out of the window over the hills and in winter it all gets covered with snow.”

Known for his cheery demeanour, Johnny Herbert needed all the positive thinking he could muster when his legs were shattered in a Formula 3000 crash in 1989. Left with a permanent limp, it didn't stop him from climbing into an F1 car barely half a year later at the Brazilian Grand Prix. In 1995, he won at Silverstone and Monza as Michael Schumacher's team-mate at Benetton. When he left Benetton at the end of the year it looked like his winning days might be over, but he took a shock victory for Stewart at the European Grand Prix in 1999. He is now one of the presenters of Sky's F1 broadcast.

Former F1 race winner and Sky F1 presenter
NATIONALITY: British

JOHNNY HERBERT

Say Cheese!

"With the Champ! This picture was taken in the Abu Dhabi paddock. It was a funny situation, Damon and I both took a picture of each other and people took pictures of us taking the picture. We work a lot together and also have fun! Over a season we spend a lot of time together and it is good to have a laugh when you can."

Damon Hill is the only son of a Formula 1 world champion to have won the world championship himself. He made his F1 debut for Brabham in 1992 while also working for Williams as a test driver that year. Following in his father Graham's footsteps he took a well-earned world championship victory for Williams in 1996 ahead of team-mate Jacques Villeneuve after finishing second in the two previous seasons. A fan favourite he twice won the BBC Sports Personality of the Year award. He retired from F1 at the end of 1999 and is currently one of the presenters on Sky Sports' F1 broadcast.

1996 F1 world champion and Sky F1 presenter
NATIONALITY: British

DAMON HILL

Rolling Back the Years

"This was taken after the Canadian GP Montreal. We were winding down from the race. We were so close to the Rolling Stones. They were superb too. A great night. Maybe the last time? I don't know. I was with the Sky F1 presentation team and Martin Donnelly and Johnny Herbert, my old racing mates. So that made it an even more memorable evening..."

Lite

For many people, James Hunt was the archetypal racing driver – fast, glamorous and dramatic. Such is his popularity that the story of his battle with Niki Lauda to win the 1976 world championship was turned into a Hollywood movie, *Rush*, in 2013. Known for his skill on track, his playboy lifestyle and his witty race commentary once he retired from driving, his legacy is being continued by his sons,Tom and Freddie, and his younger brother, David, who have launched a range of retro themed merchandise and the charitable James Hunt Foundation in his memory.

1976 world champion
NATIONALITY: British

JAMES HUNT'S FAMILY

A Champion in His Prime

“We actually have very few personal photographs of Dad but I think this one's a cracker. It was taken in the mid 1970s by his late brother, Peter 'Norm' Hunt, who was his manager throughout his F1 career. Sadly with Norm no longer around the story behind it has gone forever, but I guess that leaves a certain mystery around it which is quite nice.”

Tom Hunt

ANT SINISTRO

MUBADALA
V-Power

GULF AIR

Nick Mason is best known as the drummer in rock band Pink Floyd and is the only member of the band to have featured on every one of their albums, which have sold more than 250 million copies worldwide. However, his favourite pastime has always been fast cars and the royalties from Pink Floyd's album sales have helped him build up an enviable collection of sportscars, including his beloved Ferrari 250 GTO, one of only 39 ever built. He has also raced in various series, with the highlight of his racing career coming through five appearances in the 24 Hours of Le Mans, where he finished 18th in 1979.

Pink Floyd drummer and F1 fan

NATIONALITY: British

NICK MASON

On the Grid “Michael Schumacher at the 2006 Bahrain Grand Prix.”

Adrian Newey is widely recognised as one of the greatest designers in the history of Formula 1. He first came to the attention of the racing world when, at the age of just 25, he designed the car which won the 1984 Indianapolis 500. In F1 his designs for the Leyton House team caught the attention of Williams, who hired him in 1990. His cars powered the team to five constructors' championships and four drivers' title before he quit for McLaren where his car won both titles in 1998. He joined Red Bull Racing in 2006 and the team won both championships for four consecutive years between 2010 and 2013.

Red Bull Racing technical director
NATIONALITY: British

ADRIAN NEWEY

On the Road "This was taken when I was on a classic car rally in Sardinia."

Although Suzi Perry made her first appearance as a presenter of Formula 1 coverage in early 2013, she was already well-known to motorsport fans due to her 13-year stint presenting MotoGP coverage for the BBC. Her cheerful and friendly presenting style made her a favourite with viewers and helped to launch her onto the F1 grid and made her the first woman ever to head-up F1 coverage in the UK full-time. She has presented a wide variety of sports during her career, including the Olympics, the London Marathon, the Epsom Derby and Wimbledon. However, outside motor racing she is best known as one of the presenters of *The Gadget Show*.

BBC F1 presenter
NATIONALITY: British

SUZI PERRY

Making Friends

“A 'groupie!' taken of my BBC crew at the Austin GP. My cameraman Iain was pleased with his photo of Matt LeBlanc so that's on his phone screen! MLB is remotely photo bombing us ;-) The Lone Star State played host to a fabulous event, live music everywhere and terrific weather.”

Michael Schumacher is the most successful driver in the history of Formula 1. He has won seven world championships – two with Benetton and five for Ferrari, and more than any other driver – and set a string of other records including most wins, most pole positions and the highest number of races won in a single season (13 in 2004). Although he initially retired from F1 in 2006, the lure of racing at the top level of the sport proved too much for him and he returned in 2010 at the wheel of Mercedes' new car. He finally retired at the end of 2012.

Seven-time F1 world champion
NATIONALITY: German

MICHAEL SCHUMACHER

Lake Geneva

"This one is a shot of Lake Geneva from out of a train, coming back from a sponsorship event in Zürich for Navyboot."

VIA
PENSIONE
RISTORANTE
BELSITO

Susie Wolff is one of the few female racing drivers in the world who have driven at some of the highest levels of the sport. She started out in single seater racing in 2001, when she competed in Formula Renault. She was selected as the British Racing Drivers' Club Rising Star of the Year before moving on to Formula Three. However, she would become known for competing in the DTM German touring car series where she raced between 2006 and 2012 before she joined Williams as the team's development driver. She is married to the Mercedes executive director, Toto Wolff.

Williams development driver
NATIONALITY: British

SUSIE WOLFF

The Best Day of My Life

"I got married in Capri, a small island off the south Italian coast, and this was a folk group from the island who met me as I left the church and walked me through the streets playing traditional music. I love the vibrant colours they wear and the happiness you can see in their faces. As a racing driver, many people presume I am a tomboy but my wedding day was without a doubt the best day of my life."

'Marble collecting'. On the closing lap, drivers circuit the track and pick up rubber that has been shredded off the tyres during the race.
Photo taken on a Nikon D4 by Hidehiko Tanaka, President of Nikon UK Ltd.